# plants are magic

## VOLUME 3

Published by Rebecca Desnos

I'm Rebecca Desnos—a natural dyer,
writer and independent publisher in the
UK. I started *Plants Are Magic* magazine
in 2017. It's a magazine for plant lovers
about creating things with plants.

*Plants Are Magic* is ad-free and
supported by you. Thank you for
keeping the magazine alive!

# HELLO AND WELCOME!

'Time' is the theme for the third edition of Plants Are Magic. As a botanical dyer and seasonal creative, Time is a recurring theme in my life. I work with gifts from nature and my colour palette changes throughout the year. For me, the spring and summer are all about dyeing with the abundant offerings from nature, and then things quieten down towards the end of the year as winter approaches. For many of us, the colder months can be the perfect time to make things with the dyed fibres, pressed flowers or other botanical gifts that we have accumulated during the year. Then when spring returns, we begin the cycle once more.

Over the last 12 months, since my second baby was born, I've found that my dyeing process has slowed down more than ever to match the slower pace of my own life. I simmer flowers and leaves for just a few minutes on a very gentle heat and allow the colour to seep into the water over the next day or two. With this renewed perspective, we can sometimes find new colours — until this year my nettle dye has never been so green! Even if I only find the time to dye small swatches of fabric, little-by-little my collection of coloured linen squares will grow. I enjoy recording the passage of time on fabric and these squares will all be hand stitched into a quilt — very slowly!

The next 100 pages or so are packed full of stories, ideas and tutorials from a diverse range of makers, artists and gardeners who are all inspired by the passage of time in one way or another. I hope you find some fresh ideas within these pages. Sometimes it can be the smallest of seeds that grow into the most rewarding projects in the long term. That's my dream for this magazine — to plant some seeds and you develop and nurture some of the ideas. You just never know where they will lead! I'd love to hear if you try anything from the magazine, so do keep in touch.

Hope you enjoy the magazine,

Rebecca x

**Do you have any comments about this magazine or suggestions for future issues? I'd love to hear from you!**

*info@rebeccadesnos.com*

# Contents

"Let's take our hearts
for a walk in the woods
and listen to the magic
whispers of old trees."

— unknown

# Some of the folks who helped make this magazine

**Kim Deans** is a biodynamic lifestyle farmer and permaculturalist who lives on a small farm in Australia and also works in agricultural education and coaching. Kim gives us an introduction to biodynamic growing on page 16. *biodynamiclife.com*

**The Far Woods** is an arthouse founded by Sonya and Nina Montenegro who collaborate to create art that serves as educational tools and inspiration for reconnection to nature, food, and community. See their lunar illustration on page 16. *thefarwoods.com*

**Bonnie Rubrecht** is a writer and illustrator living on the Central Coast of California. She loves working in the dirt and all things botanical. Read Bonnie's article on the seasonality of tea on page 27. *littlegreenblackbird.co*

**Mirta Arbini** is an artist, illustrator and maker who lives in a tiny village on the banks of Lake Como, Italy. Mirta's beautiful illustrations are on pages 26 and 29. *modernbotanics.com*

**Erika Molnar** is passionate about colour which can be seen in her work as a natural dyer (read her article on goldenrod dye on page 32) and quilt-maker. She works with designers to build beautiful, repeatable naturally-dyed colourways and creates quilts that often evoke a sense of place and time through colour and form. *erikabmolnar.com*

**Heather Borkowski** is a plant whisperer, kitchen alchemist, and creative explorer who lives near the Ochil Hills in Scotland. She loves having her hands in the soil (read her article on page 35) and is passionate about helping others reconnect with nature and seasonal rhythms. *heatherborkowski.com*

**Eliza Bratton** is an artist who connects deeply with 'nature spirit' through painting and visual storytelling. Her illustrations (see one on page 34) come from realms of inner peace and guidance, often conveying messages or stories from Earth's roots and beyond. *instagram.com/onepaintedsun*

**Ocean Rose Fashakin** is a botanical dyer, mother, artist and knitter living in London. Read Ocean's inspiring story recalled from her childhood on page 39. *instagram.com/ocean_bythesea*

**Naina Bajaria** practices as an Ayurvedic lifestyle consultant and yoga teacher in the UK. She is passionate about expressing creativity and exploring spirituality by attuning to nature's rhythms. Read her article on page 42. *instagram.com/nainabajaria*

**Ellie Beck** is a textile artist, maker and storyteller living in the rainforest in NSW, Australia. She runs creative workshops in person and online. Ellie writes about creative seasons (page 48) and a special magnolia tree (page 103). *petalplum.com.au*

**Alice Griffin** lives, creates and writes from her home in North Yorkshire, UK. She loves to learn from nature, and apart from her backyard olive tree, she plans to discover many more plants that call to her soul in her new, more rooted life (read her article on page 52). *alicegriffin.co.uk*

**Herbal Academy** is an online international herbal school that teaches the art and science of plant medicine whilst honouring our intrinsic connection to nature. Learn how to do a simple tea meditation on page 56. *theherbalacademy.com*

**Tara Rose** is a writer and prolific self-taught artist. In recent years, she has developed her own soul-intuitive method of gathering knowledge and nurturing a connection with plants close to her home. Tara Rose interviews Maurizio Leo (page 62) and Raphaëlle Gagnon (page 73).

**Eleonora Matarrese**, a forager since her childhood, is a wild food expert and consultant, and runs courses on wild cooking. She opened Pikniq, the first wild food restaurant in Italy. Find her fermenting recipes on page 68. *www.lacucinadelbosco.wordpress.com*

**Lindsay Buck,** a landscape architect by trade, is passionate about the intersection of art and science, which has been a driving force in both her career and her Freshly Pressed herbarium project. Read Lindsay's story on page 83 and learn how you can start your own herbarium. *freshlypressed.ch*

**Ginny Farquhar** is a plant dyer, maker and allotment gardener. She lives in Hampshire, in the UK, and works as a sewing and community crafts tutor. Read Ginny's story about her mother's goldenrod on page 88 and how this inspired her own dyeing. *instagram.com/myrtle_sweet*

**Samorn Sanixay** is a weaver, textile designer and passionate gardener. See her natural dyeing tutorial on page 90. Samorn is the cofounder of Eastern Weft, a weaving cooperative based in Vientiane, Laos, which supports disadvantaged young Hill Tribe women through art or weaving. *easternweft.com*

**Desiree Bell** is a vegetarian and certified in herbal studies and aromatherapy. She celebrates plants for crafts, décor, food, wellness, and pure enjoyment on her blog *Botanical Lifestyle*. Learn how to make paper on page 94. *botanicallifestyle.com*

**Louise Gale** is a British mixed media artist who creates in her studio on the sunny south coast of Spain. She loves to combine the healing power of nature with the meditative process of mandala creating. Learn how to develop flower motifs on page 98 and find out more about Louise's book *Botanical Mandalas* here: *botanicalmandalas.com*

Photo by Kelly Sikkema

"*Raise your words, not voice. It is rain that grows flowers, not thunder.*"

— Rumi

# TIME TO GARDEN

*Interview by Rebecca Desnos*
*Photos by Jai Bess*

In conversation with Jai Bess.
*"Gardening is meditative; it is a mindless, repetitive form of creativity. Focusing on pulling out teensy weeds, on planting seeds to the right depth and spotting stealthy caterpillars [...] unfailingly, I relax. The space from art means I can find unexpected patterns and imagery, things that truly come from me and my space."*

**Hi Jai. Can you tell us a bit about yourself?**

My name is Jai (said like the letter 'J'). I am a printmaker, mother, very amateur gardener and chicken-obsessive living in a small house just outside of Bristol.

Whilst I put printmaking first in that list, realistically with a one year old and a four year old in the house, I have to steal moments where I can! But when I am not in my workroom, we can either be found in the kitchen or in the garden.

**Did you grow up surrounded by nature?**

Growing up it was just my mother, brother and I living in a tiny house in the middle of nowhere. Out the front were endless fields and out the back was woodland. It felt very sheltered from the rest of the world. My mother

was a potter and worked from a small shed in the garden whilst my brother and I spent hours in the garden making dens and digging for treasures behind the chicken coop. My mother was a fantastic gardener and would spend hours tending her vegetables. All my strongest childhood memories are of us all in that outside space. That said, as a child I had no patience for planting and growing. I spent my days bug hunting and building nests for mice and birds (who, ungratefully, never once moved into my creations).

Despite my impatience with vegetable growing, I can see the influence of this in all aspects of my life now—in how we eat, the hobbies and interests we have, the flock of chickens that complete our family, in my garden and in the contents of my sketchbooks.

HUMAN THAT
GROWS FOOD

**Can you tell us about your little piece of paradise in your back garden?**

In reality, my garden is a scrubby little space—we live in a boxy 1960s ex-council house, overlooked by flats and the ground is a terrible clay. But in the summer months it transforms into something magical. The peas and squashes climb, the nasturtiums spill out of the raised beds and cover the mud, the tomatoes tumble off the window sills hiding the cracked plastic.

Evening after evening, I sit on the doorstep with a cup of tea (or glass of wine) in hand, watching my garden until the sun fades or the baby cries. In these hours even the cabbage white butterflies seem charming.

I once heard on the radio that a garden is 'time manifest'—that to garden presumes a future. At a time when things feel uncertain, there is something wonderful about a garden. I think about what grew last year, what might grow this year and how that might change my garden next year. In the winter, when my enthusiasm wanes and I put off kneeling in the mud and guiltily ignore the last of the summer jobs I failed to complete, there is something wondrous in stewing borlotti beans and remembering the harvest, or taking frozen apples from the freezer to make a winter crumble. In my day to day life I am not a patient person, but in my garden I become a human capable of planting Honesty flowers one spring, knowing I won't get the dried bunch until the end of the following summer.

> "I ONCE HEARD
> ON THE RADIO
> THAT A GARDEN
> IS 'TIME
> MANIFEST' –
> THAT TO GARDEN
> PRESUMES A
> FUTURE."

**Can you tell us how your garden is an inspiration for your art?**

It is impossible not to be inspired by a garden. I spend so long staring at each stage that the images are fixed in my mind. From bare soil, to seedlings, to plants, to redirecting the beans that always climb the wrong way or waiting for courgette flowers to appear, then harvesting and gathering, whilst removing opportunistic slugs and woodlice. Each stage is so slow and I wait with anticipation, checking daily. How could those things not tip into sketchbooks? Last year I lived and breathed beetroots! It was my first year growing them—we grew three different colours. I waited weeks for them to start bulking out, then overnight it felt like all we could eat were beetroots. I found I wanted to add a beetroot motif to everything I created.

12

### How does gardening nourish your creativity?

Like many people, I struggle somewhat to switch off from social media. The sheer scope of 'inspirational' content becomes stifling. Why even begin when so much beautiful work already exists? Or worse is flicking through my sketchbook and realising that my ideas are no longer coming from my own imaginings, but from the works of other artists.

Gardening is meditative; it is a mindless, repetitive form of creativity. Focusing on pulling out teensy weeds, on planting seeds to the right depth and spotting stealthy caterpillars, my thoughts stop obsessing and, unfailingly, I relax. The space from art means I can find

unexpected patterns and imagery, things that truly come from me and my space.

My chickens are the funniest of ginger ladies. A blank page is rarely intimidating, as doodling the girls can always break it up, then drawings can leak comfortably into the rest of it.

I'm very much a novice gardener. I refer to books (or my mother) constantly and I rely heavily on the knowledge and experience of those around me. In gardening, I am not trying to stand out in a sea of other gardens, I am trying to understand how it works and what my role is in that. That revelation has helped me understand printmaking in a different way. I don't need to stand out, what I need is to understand my craft and how I can use it.

## How did you learn the art of printing?

I first discovered block printing whilst at university. I wasn't exactly sailing through my academic career at the time. I had failed and left behind the degree that I had believed for years was to be my life's vocation (truly a good thing—I would have made a terrible doctor) and was undertaking a second degree to stave off, unsuccessfully, the feelings of failure.

I was feeling pretty lost. Then, for my birthday, my wonderful partner bought me all the basic tools for lino printing. I sat on the bed, leaning on a textbook and got stuck in.

My first print was a terrible mountain and map scene. I ambitiously included some text on it which I forgot to reverse. It was terrible, but I was hooked. Block printing took root.

For me it has taken a lot of time to learn. It never occurred to me to buy a book on print making—not till much later. It has all been trial and error: shoddy tools, inappropriate inks, absurd paper choices. I think I had been pulling prints for over a year before I invested in actual print-making paper.

Until I found printmaking, I had been guilty of getting carried away with each new interest, buying new kit and devices only to find my enthusiasm waning. But I knew with *this* I had found something different and there was no rush. This way, all my time and energy was spent learning how to design and think in terms of blocks and developing my ability to carve. The other stuff came later. I feel I understand this craft much better for the time and trials I've poured into it. The tools and techniques I use, I use because I know they work for me, not because someone has told me it is what's best.

## Growing up, did your mum create any traditions surrounding nature that you carry through to the present day with your own children?

My mother instilled the importance of tradition in us from a young age—her enthusiasm for the small things is thrillingly contagious.

Whilst I was pregnant with my first, who was due in the winter months, I inevitably spent a lot of time imagining what Christmas would look like no longer as the child, but as the provider of the festivities. But, like many people I know, I find the reality of the excess and overwhelm of Christmas jarring in comparison to the rest of my parenting.

Despite my son's young age, the talk had already — inevitably, it feels — focused on what he might get. I felt sad that year that the magic was getting confused with a shopping list.

So this year, more than ever, we've decided to celebrate the magic throughout the year.

We are seeking out and learning about traditions and celebrations to mark throughout the seasons. Burn's night has always been part of our calendar, and we always greet the solstices with food, candles and wine (in the garden, or cosy in the warmth depending on the season). But new to me this year so far is Imbolc and Wassailing.

In the middle of January we did a Wassailing for our apple tree. Once the baby was asleep, we went into the dark of our garden, dressed up against the drizzle and woke our tree with a poem to the beat of a four year old with a saucepan and wooden spoon. We gave the tree toast and apple juice and spent a while discussing all the things we would do with the apples she might grow us.

I want my children to feel the excitement in the first blackberry picking (and subsequent crumble) of the year, the first apples on the tree and the hunts for snowdrops. All these things feel just as worthy of celebration as the official holidays. 🌿

*To see more of Jai's art, visit:*

*- instagram.com/jaibess*
*- etsy.com/shop/jaibirdpress*

"...THIS YEAR, MORE THAN EVER, WE'VE DECIDED TO CELEBRATE THE MAGIC THROUGHOUT THE YEAR."

# GARDENING WITH THE MOON

### How and why to attune your garden to the lunar cycles

*Words & photo by Kim Deans*
*Illustration by The Far Woods - Sonya & Nina Montenegro*

As a biodynamic grower, I have spent many years exploring moon planting guides to help us choose the most appropriate times for carrying out activities in our garden and on our small farm. At first, this method of growing felt overwhelming as there was a huge amount of information on the biodynamic calendar. How was it possible to do everything in the limited amount of time we had? Over the years we found ways to implement more and more of the principles. There are still times when something happens regardless of the timings on the calendar, but the difference now is that we have the tools available to us to make a considered and conscious choice.

Since attuning our farming to the moon cycles and Mother Earth's natural rhythms, we have felt a subtle energetic shift in our landscape and the vitality of our plants. The work we do in our garden and landscape now feels like it flows more and it is less of a chore as we connect with a force greater than ourselves. Growing plants in this way nurtures our relationship with the cosmos and nature's rhythms.

Living in tune with the cycles of the moon – and growing plants in this way – was part of traditional culture for centuries. The advent of electric lighting has led to our modern civilisation disconnecting from these natural rhythms as modern conveniences have reduced our awareness of them. If you live in the countryside you will have a better view of the sky and moon at night, but if you're a city dweller you will find it much harder to see the constellations and notice the moon amidst bright city lights.

The effects of the moon phases are most noticeable in the tidal rhythms of the oceans. These tidal rhythms make it obvious how moonlight is deeply connected to water. Considering our soils, plants and animals (including humans) all contain and are dependent upon water, it is obvious that moon cycles will impact life on Earth much further than the tidal rhythms. Plants are strongly influenced by lunar cycles as the amount of sunlight reflected back to Earth by the moon changes through the month. Due to the influence of the moon on water, the moon cycle has a greater impact on soil and plants when conditions are wet and soil is saturated than when conditions are dry. It has also become evident that modern agricultural practices dependent upon artificial fertilisers and poisonous chemicals will deaden the soil and correspondingly reduce the plants' sensitivity and responsiveness to the moon cycles.

"...WE HAVE FELT A SUBTLE ENERGETIC SHIFT IN OUR LANDSCAPE AND THE VITALITY OF OUR PLANTS."

# A moon planting guide

I recommend using this introductory guide which I have illustrated opposite. It will guide and show you the ideal timings for planting according to the four stages of the moon. This basic system is based upon the ebb and flow of the plant's sap in tune with the rhythms of the moon.

## Waxing moon phase

Light is increasing towards a full moon and sap flow is drawn upwards. This is the most suitable time for sowing and transplanting leafy, flowering and fruiting annual crops. It is also a good time for applying liquid fertilisers, pruning and grafting as increased sap flow produces new growth more quickly. The first quarter of the waxing moon is most suited to leafy annuals and the quarter leading up to the full moon is most suited to flowering and fruiting annuals.

## Waning moon phase

Light is decreasing as the moon changes from a full to a new moon and the sap flow is drawn downwards. Energy flows towards the roots, which makes this the most suitable time for planting root crops and perennial plants that live longer than two years. It also a good time for applying solid fertilisers, taking cuttings, dividing plants, pruning dormant plants and harvesting. The last quarter phase as the moon approaches the new moon is a time to avoid planting and focus on soil improvement through activities such as weeding, mulching, composting and cultivating. If you wish

to reduce vigorous regrowth of rampant plants then pruning at this time will be beneficial.

## Transitions

Avoid sowing, planting and pruning during the 12 hours before and after the transition time from one phase to the next and use this time to work on improving your soil instead.

## Cosmic forces

We started with this simple four-phase model and gradually added to this as we learnt to implement more details from a more complex calendar. Biodynamic calendars provide additional information regarding moon-related timings including moon opposition Saturn, ascending and descending moon, lunar perigee and apogee, as well as nodes and rhythms of the moon's path through the constellations. Biodynamic farmers and gardeners work with the rhythms of the moon, planets & constellations of the zodiac, recognising that plants grow not only through the fertility of the soil but also with the support of the cosmos.

Biodynamics is a way of enlivening the earth so that cosmic energies can stream into the soil and it fosters the connection between all living things and the cosmos. Consciously working with these cosmic formative forces and applying this knowledge in making and using biodynamic preparations is one of the distinguishing features of biodynamic growing.

## The Basic Biodynamic System

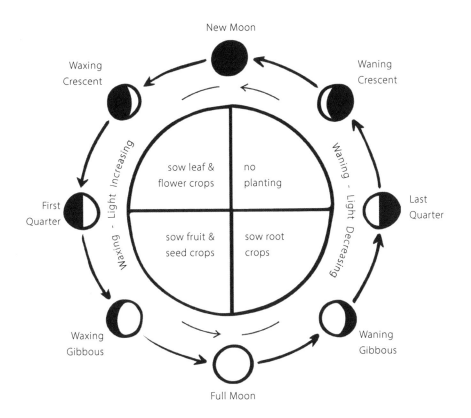

"THIS BASIC SYSTEM IS BASED UPON THE EBB AND FLOW OF THE PLANT'S SAP IN TUNE WITH THE RHYTHMS OF THE MOON."

# A more detailed approach

If you wish to move beyond the basic moon planting guide, you may choose to implement some of these growing and harvesting principles.

When you begin your biodynamic growing journey, it can be helpful to begin with just one thing and build up from there. Learn and observe as you go and have fun. I like to plan things in my personal diary so I don't need to keep looking at my biodynamic calendar. This simplifies things and keeps me focused. If you look to buy a biodynamic calendar, ensure that you purchase the correct one for your hemisphere. 

"BIODYNAMICS IS A WAY OF ENLIVENING THE EARTH SO THAT COSMIC ENERGIES CAN STREAM INTO THE SOIL..."

| Phase | Focus |
|---|---|
| **Full Moon** | Avoid harvesting.<br>48 hours before is a good time to sow seeds and apply liquid manures |
| **New Moon** | No gardening work the day before.<br>Avoid sowing seeds.<br>A good time to fell timber. |
| **Moon Opposition Saturn** | Good time for planting, transplanting and applying Biodynamic Preparation 501 (Horn silica) |
| **Ascending Moon**<br>The moon's arc is getting higher in the sky. | Good time for applying Biodynamic Preparation 501 (Horn silica), sowing seeds, grafting, hay cutting, applying foliar nutrients, taking cuttings for propagation, harvesting fruits, leaves and flowers. |
| **Descending Moon**<br>The moon's arc is getting lower in the sky. | Good time for applying Biodynamic Preparation 500 (Horn Manure), composting, cultivation, transplanting, applying soil nutrients, pruning, harvesting roots. |
| **Node**<br>The point where the moon crosses the sun's path. | Avoid agricultural and horticultural activities 6 hours either side of a node. |
| **Perigee**<br>The point where the moon is closest to the Earth. | Stress Period.<br>Avoid sowing seeds 12 hours either side of perigee. |
| **Apogee**<br>The point where the moon is furthest from the Earth. | Stress Period.<br>Avoid sowing seeds 12 hours either side of Apogee, with the exception of potatoes which are good to plant now. |
| **Moon in Earth Constellations**<br>Taurus, Virgo, Capricorn | A good time to plant or work on root crops. |
| **Moon in Water Constellations**<br>Cancer, Scorpio, Pisces | A good time to plant or work on leafy crops. |
| **Moon in Air Constellations**<br>Gemini, Libra, Aquarius | A good time to plant or work on flower crops. |
| **Moon in Fire Constellations**<br>Aries, Leo, Sagittarius | A good time to plant or work on fruit crops. |

# FROM SEED TO CLOTH

*Interview by Rebecca Desnos*
*Photos by Jennifer Dennis*

Imagine growing your own fabric from seed!
Jennifer Dennis, a gardener and knitter, tells us
how she grows cotton plants for fibre.

**How did you get started growing cotton?**

To some extent gardening was passed down to me, or at the very least encouraged. My mother figured out early on that the best way to keep my sister and me from messing with her vegetables was to give us our own raised beds where we could grow whatever we wanted.

Right now I'm growing cotton on a very small scale in an 8 x 12' community garden plot that I share "custody" of with another community garden member. She happens to be a master gardener and has an interest in growing less common plants for demonstration purposes, and I like growing less common plants for the learning experience.

**We tend to think of cotton as a white fibre but it actually grows in different colours. Can you tell us more about this?**

Cotton grows in a range of colours, the most common being white, brown/tan, and green. It used to grow in even more colours like pink and blue but those have been lost to antiquity. The colour does depend on the variety of the cotton grown, and can vary in intensity and colourfastness even within the variety. Sally Fox of Vreseis in California is doing some amazing work with organic cotton breeding to stabilise and broaden the range of cotton colours.

### Can you tell us a bit about growing cotton?

Cotton, like all plants, has certain environments that it prefers and different varieties do well in different environments. It's also a heavy feeding plant so requires lots of nutrients and/or a rich soil.

Cotton is technically a perennial but it doesn't tolerate the cold so is often treated as an annual, which also helps with pest control. In zones 8-10 it can be sewn directly outside and it may survive the winter. In USDA zones 5-7 (I'm in zone 6) cotton is generally treated like tomatoes: started indoors and transplanted outside after the threat of frost is gone. That said, last year we direct seeded our cotton and it did fine, we just didn't have all the bolls ripen before the plants were killed by frost.

If you don't live in the ideal environment for growing cotton, you can still grow it in large pots in a greenhouse. Cotton does need direct sun to do well though.

### How do you process the fibre?

Once the cotton bolls are ripe (when they have fully opened and the cotton is dry) I remove them from the plant. Then I pull the cotton and seeds out of the boll and sort them by colour. I remove the seeds and save some for the following year. The rest of it I process on a small crank gin, which goes a bit faster. I use my cotton cards (brushes) to brush the cotton into alignment and using a sanded bamboo skewer roll it into punis

# "...TO LOOK AT A PIECE OF FABRIC AND SEE THE PLANT THAT GREW IT, SMELL THE EARTH THAT NURTURED THE PLANT... IT'S A WONDERFUL FEELING."

to spin - though sometimes I skip this step and spin it straight from the "cloud".

**Where did you learn to spin fibres and what is your preferred spinning method for cotton?**

The first fibre I learned to spin was wool. I have a friend who spins, so I learned from her, from books, and from the Internet. I started spinning cotton as a personal challenge since I had heard it was a difficult fibre.

My favourite method for spinning cotton is on supported spindles. Since the weight of the spindle rests on a surface I'm able to spin a much finer yarn than I would otherwise. I also spin cotton on very light drop spindles and on a special wheel called a Charkha. The spindles are not as fast as the wheel, but there's

something meditative about using them.

**There is such a story behind each of your knitted pieces, as you've grown the fibre from seed. How does it make you feel?**

I love it. I love it so much. To be able to look at a piece of fabric and see the plant that grew it, smell the earth that nurtured the plant, feel the sun that fed the plant — it's a wonderful feeling. I know exactly what went into the piece of cloth, from seed to finished product; there's such an interconnectedness there that's hard to put into words but is so powerful.

At the same time there is very much a feeling of independence - similar to the one I get when I grow my own food or make something from scratch.

The other thing it makes me feel? *Grateful.* Grateful not only that I have the opportunity and the ability to grow my own fabric, but also grateful that I don't have to, that I can use cotton towels and wear cotton jeans without having to grow, harvest, process and make them myself. The number of hours that goes into a home-grown piece of fabric when the weeding and picking and ginning and spinning and weaving/knitting are all added up is more than I ever thought it would be. I now understand why sheets were once mentioned in wills and passed down through the family. 🌿

*To find out more about Jennifer's cotton growing and processing, visit:*

*- instagram.com/expnumber1*
*- experimentnumberone.wordpress.com*

# GROWING
# SEASONAL TEA

*Words & interview by Bonnie Rubrecht*
*Illustrations by Mirta Arbini*

Bonnie Rubrecht talks to Laura Hamill who runs Perenial Collective—a company that creates seasonal tea blends.

The concept of seasonality has caught on in recent years, with the onset of farm-to-table restaurants and the reemerging popularity of small-scale farming. Yet most of us prefer to live in the evergreen reality of now that allows us the freedom to eat strawberries in December—we live in an increasingly seasonless world. Perhaps it is for this reason the idea of limited availability, whether sun-warmed flowering herbs or vine-ripened tomatoes, kindles such a feeling of luxury. Similarly, in our lives besot with busyness, stopping to take the time for a moment of presence can feel intensely indulgent. Reflection is something we often neglect, overwhelmed by errands and to-do lists.

Tea, once its own kind of currency due to its immense stature in a world of limits, holds its own kind of furtive appeal,

beckoning back to times that allowed for contemplation and conversation with those we know and love. Based on this element of ritual, the creator of Perennial Collective ("Perennial"), a nascent seasonal tea company, saw an opportunity.

Laura Hamill is both a remarkable cook and farmer. I was lucky enough to stay at her historic home in Lambertville, New Jersey overlooking the Delaware River on a rocky outcrop near the wooded Amwell Sourlands. Owing to her background in culinary arts, Laura has a broad-based love for local fruit and vegetables, and heritage foods in particular. *"The summer after I finished my undergrad in 2010, I started my first herbal garden at my mom's farm, Stonybrook Meadows, in New Jersey. I was working as a line cook at* Elements, *a farm-to-table restaurant, and the level of* food we were putting out captivated me. I started the garden on land that had been used for grazing; it was a nod to my degree in environmental studies, and reaffirmed my underlying belief that we can steward our land more thoughtfully." In creating a simple perennial garden, Laura found a way to balance the long hours working in the kitchen. "All the herbs I planted were very gentle—elderberry, lemon balm, calendula, nasturtium, mint."

Laura's love for herbal farming grew with her experience, and she later began growing herbs in her sister-in-law's flower garden at Rolling Hills Farm. "I wanted to focus on nervine, calming, female balancing herbs. We grow skullcap, chamomile, motherwort, red raspberry, echinacea, black cohosh, valerian, lavender, rose, among others," Laura says.

# LAURA HARVESTS FROM HER OWN GARDENS IN THE MORNING "AS THE SUN BEGINS TO CHASE AWAY THE DEW."

Time is an elusive, circuitous thing: we find ourselves always lamenting our lack of it, without actually making an effort to change the circumstances that deprive us of it. One of the important aspects of farming is the inability to rush the process. Growing plants from seed to stem requires a great measure of patience, in sharp contrast with our lives spangled with social media and instant gratification.

Growing herbs for the purposes of creating tea requires diligence, but also awareness of the potency and medicinal qualities the plants are harvested for. It is a very different kind of agriculture. "Medicinal plants share a similarity to wine grapes," Laura points out. "The less comfortable you make their home, the more work they have to do, and the more potent they become. The highest medicinal value for plants is almost always in the wild because they're under more pressure." The renewed interest in wild botanicals is not without problems, and overzealous foragers sometimes deplete natural availability and diversity in their enthusiasm. "I am cautious about what is being wild-harvested and prefer to use organically cultivated herbs for the majority of our tea," Laura acknowledges. "There can be a nice balance met on land that's been altered by humans, but that naturally reseeds – like foraging for yarrow on conserved parcels of friends' land."

Laura harvests from her own gardens in the morning "as the sun begins to chase away the dew." She describes the cyclical nature of the plants' yearly cycles, mirrored in their daily cycle. "In spring energy is moved outward into shoots and foliage, in summer it is invested in blossoms and fruit, come fall it's directed down to root systems, and in winter there is dormancy. There is also a daily cycle as the sun evaporates water out of the leaves and blossoms." She emphasises the importance of timing in her work. *"You have to remember plants are always respiring, even after they are cut. I try to get them into the dehydrator as soon as possible, before they have a chance to wilt. Keeping them out of direct sunlight is key."*

Challenges abound. Too much snow, not enough water. Inclement weather generally can create tremendous issues for anyone trying to use sustainable growing techniques. While we have evolved to make commercial farming more efficient and less unpredictable, the sheer complexity of relying solely on the elements teaches humility and resilience. One must adapt to succeed in cultivating a herbal garden. Nature will not be hurried. *"I've been overzealous with pruning,"* Laura admits, describing what she has learned out in the field. *"Each plant requires its personal touch, mimicking evolutionary codes. If you prune incorrectly it can cost you your entire harvest the next year, so each year before I prune I make a plan for each plant."*

Creating tea blends takes a seasoned palette as well as an understanding of what the market is looking for, and the artistry can make it challenging. *"I love bitter- and hay-flavoured teas—an ocean away from what the majority of the American palate favour. I'm learning to calculate this into how I plan yearly for diversity in the blends. Most blends I create working with the grower, based on* what they have available in that season and what represents their land. I want to use the most vibrant part of the plant at a given time of year. Spring blends tend to be more delicate and anise leaning. Summer is abundance and we have much more sweet flavours coming out this time of year. In fall we go back to the roots so we get heat (like in ginger) and bitter flavours."*

The concept for Perennial came out of Laura's own experience foraging for medicinals during her undergraduate studies at the University of Victoria, where she tagged along with medicinal herbalist Nadine Ijaz and others in the lush green woodlands of British Columbia. *"During the months that classes were is session, I lived in a communal house with cupboards packed full of herbs in Ball jars. There were always herbs drying near the kitchen. It became how I thought of having a pot of tea—making a blend from what we had collectively harvested and steeping it in a French press that lived on our counter."*

The ability to harvest herbs and bring them quickly to market gives small-scale farmers and herb growers an advantage Laura believes is critical for the success of her business. *"Knowing where and who the herbs were produced by, and that they were produced with the highest level of care, that's the assurance that sets the Perennial Collective apart."* Her intentionality shows through in the rough cut pieces of mint, chamomile, skullcap, a kaleidoscope of loose-leaf flowers and greens housed in light impermeable cobalt glass jars.

Laura is conscientious of the role that growers and curators of medicinal plants play. *"Herbal wellness is my vehicle for introducing the notion of stewardship to the broader public. I believe that when we learn to recognise which local weeds are edible and how nutrient dense they can be, we become aware of patterns of abundance. More subtly, we become emotionally attuned to our landscape mosaic. I hope the way we think about landscape and development begins to shift to account for ecological and social values. It sounds lofty to say aloud, but this is the foundation for Perennial's guiding values."*

Heraclitus wrote that we never step into the same river twice, and our natural world changes invariably season to season. Perennial's teas are crafted in response to what nature dictates— weather, the composition of the land and the distinct hand of the individual farmer. In herbs that flourish, the flavour and terroir in each blend is unique to just one season, one point in time. While we crave consistency and sameness, life outdoors in sun and soil and spray teaches a different lesson — one of resiliency in the face of undulating conditions and environments. It is a lesson we desperately need to be reminded of, however much we like to pretend that everything could stay exactly the same if we try hard enough. Our lives are finite, which is why it is so critical that we pay attention to the here and now, lest we miss that amazing and fleeting part of our existence: the present.

Laura's devotion to the myriad benefits that tisanes can offer and her love for the art of the process is discernable in Perennial's teas. When I tried the fall harvest tea just over a year ago, I was eager to steep several more cups. The blend evoked memories of the warmth of the garden as it rescinded into winter under a blanket of snow, requiring me to slow down and appreciate the delicate brightness and zeal of lemongrass and mint. I remembered walking with my grandmother in her California garden, rubbing spearmint leaves together and the smell that lingered afterwards in the summer sun. We each grow into our own lives out of shared experiences like these that require attention and pause. In her work with Perennial, Laura sums it up eloquently, *"After working in a variety of roles in the good food world for over a decade I finally feel that I've found my calling. There is nothing I'd rather be doing."* 🌿

*To find out more, visit: perennialcollective.com*

*"Drink your tea slowly and reverently,
as if it is the axis on which the
world earth revolves - slowly, evenly,
without rushing toward the future."*


— Thich Nhat Hanh

# COLOUR AS TERROIR*

*Words and photos by Erika Molnar*

## A sense of *time* in natural dyes.

I make colour from plants; from their stems and leaves and roots and flowers. The compounds that the plants make – to protect themselves from bugs, or mould, or deer and rabbits, or even from the sun – provide me my palette. Like grapes and wines, my madder, indigo, marigold and goldenrod provide a record of the environment and passage of time.

The summers of 2016 and 2017 were very different. One was a drought, the other was not. One was hot, the other much more moderate. Each year, I collected goldenrod from the same locations and made dye baths using the same recipe. I weighed out my plant matter, separated leaves and stems from flowers. I used the same volume of water, the same amount of heat, the same fibre.

The colours were astonishing.

We have come to expect consistent colour in textiles – we want to buy a top and have the colour look as it did online or on our friend. Petro-colour allows for this: identical, single element colours

*Top dye jar - dye made from goldenrod stems.*
*Bottom dye jar - dye from goldenrod flowers.*

* Train of thought started in conversation with Brooke Sinnes 15 years ago.

*Top swatch - dye colour from goldenrod flowers in 2016, the year of the drought. Bottom swatch - colour from flowers in 2017.*

Home dyers were playing with the same variables. They foraged the fields looking for specific plants that they knew yielded reliable colour. As time passed, these dye recipes were included in the books called women's home companions. An old dye pamphlet reflects the iron-rich water of the area: colours are shifted towards brown and grey when the recipe uses well-water. When a bright colour is desired, rainwater is recommended.

Back to the goldenrod: in the drought year, the plants were stressed. They were protecting themselves from pests and sun in a race to make seeds. The water table was low and the groundwater was heavy with iron and manganese. Everything I dyed looks greener and browner. In the cooler, wetter year, the plants were not as stressed; the colour was clearer and more yellow. Recording colour on textiles is a fascinating way to mark the passage of time. Plant colour, like wine, has terroir.

can be produced and mixed with high consistency.

Until about 160 years ago, all textiles were dyed with plants. Master dyers were able to reproduce colour, within reason. They worked with the variations of strength in dyestuff, they knew how different sources of dye provided different shades of red, blue or yellow. They knew that indigo from India was different to indigo grown in Central America. They preferred madder from certain regions of the Middle East and Europe. They worked with the terroir of their dyes, like artists work with the palette of paints.

The resulting colours – complex and beautiful – are captured in Old Masters' paintings. You can reverse engineer the recipe for the colour of a silk dress in a portrait of a courtier from 1760. That shifting red-orange luminescence is madder. A fustic green looks very different from a weld green.

# "RECORDING COLOUR ON TEXTILES IS A FASCINATING WAY TO MARK THE PASSAGE OF TIME."

# TRANSFORMATION

*Words by Heather Borkowski*
*Illustration by Eliza Bratton*

*"Dirt is not dirt, but a teeming mass of microorganisms that turns death back into life."*

– Joyce McGreevy

In the early spring, when the snowdrops are blooming and crocuses are just starting to rise out of the ground, I open up my compost bin from the past year and sink my shovel into moist, dark, crumbly humus. Taking some in my hands, I pause, remembering last year's garden, while breathing in the earthy, sweet scent of new soil, of new possibilities.

Studded with worms and memories, bits of uncrushed eggshell and the odd avocado stone, most of what I hold in my hands has been transformed. For the composting process – whether it happens in a barrel, in your garden beds, or on the forest floor – is one of change. The old and worn are released into the ingredients to nourish something new. The process is as calm as it is grounded. It occurs in stark contrast to the quick and showy transformation of fire, which burns a pile of sticks to ash in a matter of minutes. That is not soil's way. Soil moves slowly and steadily in its bid to create change.

Some nights, beneath the light of the full moon, I slip into the garden and bury slips of paper into the Earth. On them I write ideas and patterns that I no longer want or need in my life – things that do not need instant release, but

# "SOIL IS THE EARTH'S DIGESTIVE SYSTEM AND, LIKE OUR OWN, IS FULL OF MICRO-ORGANISMS WHICH HELP PLANTS ASSIMILATE MINERALS AND NUTRIENTS."

can be broken down gently over time. I give these to the soil and ask it to hold space for their transformation. I find Earth energy to be both nourishing and nurturing; as these intentions are held in her embrace, there is a gentle slipping away rather than a dramatic release. In this leaving, a space is created for new things to sprout and grow.

## Alive

In the back corner of my garden grows a patch of comfrey and another of nettles. I love to harvest their vibrant green leaves in spring and summer and ferment them into food for the soil. For soil is alive. It combines the remains of the past with the life of the present. It includes minerals, air, water, bacteria, mycelium and organic matter working together as a giant organism. Each teaspoon holds billions of microorganisms. Without this life, soil is only the dull, dead dirt that you find on commercial farms after decades of chemical use. It is its aliveness that nourishes our plants and that needs to be nourished in turn.

Even after years of farming and gardening, it wasn't until I started studying herbalism that I really began to understand soil. Soil is the Earth's digestive system and, like our own, is full of microorganisms which help plants assimilate minerals and nutrients. In much the same way that we create a healthy microbiome in our gut by eating a diet including probiotics and prebiotics, the health of the soil can also be improved. Instead of sauerkraut or yogurt, we can feed it comfrey and compost teas. This contributes to its aliveness and helps it to remain vibrant for many seasons to come.

## Creating Place

Walking through the purple heather covered hills in late August, munching on bilberries, I know without looking or sampling, that the soil beneath my feet is acidic. These plants don't grow on chalky fields or sandy shorelines. As we become more in tune with the plant communities around us, we realise the many ways that our landscapes are shaped by the soil. Its minerals, nutrients, and pH combine with weather and climate to determine what vegetation is able to flourish.

Soil acts as a bridge between past and present, near and far, life and death. When I farmed in Italy, the Scirocco wind would bring red dust from the deserts of Africa and drop it on the land. This would mix with the weathered limestone and Pleistocene clays, raindrops carried from faraway lakes and the decay of native plants to create a soil unique to that place. No soil is exactly the same. The plants that grow on it are shaped by its make up, which like the weather, influences their flavour and constituents. This means that carrots I grow in my garden will taste ever so subtly different and have different nutrient levels than those grown in yours.

## Time

I spent my university days time travelling and solving puzzles while studying geology – moving back and forth between past and present. Time was linear in my world. I remember staring up at a cliff face from the beach below, my eyes following the alternating diagonal layers of light and dark skyward. I looked down at my boots on ground which was once an ancient sea floor, while at the top of the cliff were the present day loam-nourished summer grasses. I was fascinated with being able to see the memories of millions of years spread out before me, expressed visually in the changing colours of ancient sediments. Awed at the ways past and present could interact in one plane.

My sense of time shifted when I returned to the garden. As I spent season after season with my hands in the soil, I began to live in sync with Earth's rhythms and no longer experienced time as linear. The cycles of the moon, changes of the seasons, life and death in the garden returned again and again. Each time they brought with them both the familiar and the new. Soil is the mixing pot for cyclical time, holding the stories from the past and adding them to the present. As gardeners, we not only join into relationship with the plants that we tend, but also with the soil that we nourish, weaving our own stories into its ever evolving make up.

## Returning

I pull on my wellies and walk across the muddy garden path with my bowl of kitchen peelings. Tossing them into the barrel with a handful of leaves and a sprinkle of rock dust, I give thanks and await their transformation. 🌿

"[IN AFRICA] TREES, PLANTS
AND FLORA ARE GIFTS FROM
ANCESTORS, PASSED DOWN LIKE
BIRTHMARKS."

# GROUNDED

*Words and photo by Ocean Rose Fashakin*

When walking through lush, green foliage, I'm reminded of the connection we all have deep within. Sitting crossed-legged on the clay floor I was equal parts perplexed and fascinated by the fast-moving, earth-coloured hands. These women – pure enigmas dressed in colourful, plant dyed dresses and clinking gold jewellery – were making floor mats woven out of lengths of jute and otherwise discarded leaves. Nothing went to waste. As a teenager, these old-school relics didn't spark my attention much, but when I would sit once more at my grandmother's feet, I was flung to another time.

The cracking of the open fire was both inviting and intimidating, but there my grandma was—impossibly close to the amber flames. She was stirring a pot of soon-to-be Moin Moin—a dish packed with freshly ground black eyed peas, roasted chilli peppers, grilled onions and a sundry of other delicacies. Finally, intricately wrapped in newly-plucked banana leaves and left to slowly cook in an underground pit. Banana leaves are perfect for Moin Moin as they are waterproof, so ideal for cooking liquids.

As a child I didn't appreciate the magic going on around me, or the musical quality it gave to my life. Plants were used at almost every turn in our daily routines. Kola tree branches used to brush gleaming white teeth, shea butter to ward off wrinkles, "herbal" gins to cure ailments, vegetable based meals, bedding, housing, clothing...

Sustainability practices were seen as a symbol of grace and love in Nigeria, and certainly within the continent of Africa. It's second nature for us to not throw away nuts from fresh fruit, knowing that in some fashion they'll prove useful. Trees, plants and flora are gifts from ancestors, passed down like birthmarks. As long as family were around to tend to the fallen gifts of a new season, the benefits would take root and always be available to nurture the soul.

Mother Nature teaches lessons to the tune of balance and patience.

*"Nature does not hurry
yet everything is accomplished"*

— Lao Tzu

# AYURVEDIC SELF CARE RITUALS

*Words and photos by Naina Bajaria*

Ayurveda is a 5000 year old system of natural healing that originates from India. It is a science of life: *Ayur = life, Veda = science or knowledge.* Ayurveda recognises that human beings are part of nature and offers ways to help us rebalance our bodies for optimum well being. Try implementing an Ayurvedic daily routine - *Dinacharya* - to reconnect to the Earth's rhythm and feel more energised during the day and sleep better at night.

Over the last few years, my study and practice of yoga and Ayurveda have enabled me to truly understand the power of experiential learning. Despite the enormity of these topics, much of the conceptual knowledge weaved into them can be self-realised in the practice of a daily routine.

Attending a yoga class or seeing an Ayurvedic physician can be a beneficial experience for anyone, however I am becoming more passionate in understanding that it is the qualities that you take into your life after such experiences that truly matter the most. By having what is known Ayurvedically as 'Dinacharya' (an Ayurvedic daily routine), we can practice and cultivate an awareness of our body and mind everyday which can have a lasting and sustainable impact on our wellbeing.

The Dinacharya also enables us to foster a connection to the natural world by harmonising our activities with the Earth's rhythms. It builds a healthy habitual practice of self-care to

our body which translates into life in numerous ways. With the application and ingestion of nature's gifts, we are directly connecting to what is a part of us. In Ayurvedic philosophy, plants are made up of varying quantities of each of the five elements—ether, air, fire, water and earth—as is everything in existence. By recognising this, we can function harmoniously with life, enabling us to feel unity and connection rather than separation and individualisation.

## Rising

Ideally, we should wake between 4:00 and 6:00 because the elements of ether and air are more prominent around us. This creates lift in our bodies and enables us to get up more easily. It also creates movement and so it is a good time to eliminate wastes from the body.

In the yogic texts, this time in the morning is also known as Brahma Murtha. It is a time of purity within the air, so a short meditation practice or reflection time is ideal.

Drink some warm water to cleanse the organs, then brush your teeth and include tongue scraping to rid toxins from the mouth.

The sunrise is a very powerful time of the day and performing some yoga postures such as the sun salutation is an ideal way to stretch and awaken the physical body without requiring too much time. As the sun rises, we rise too, and when we appreciate and connect to this, we can understand our part in the universe.

> "IT BUILDS A HEALTHY HABITUAL PRACTICE OF SELF-CARE TO OUR BODY..."

# Cleansing the skin

Now we can take time to bathe. Try making an ubtan which is a powdered mix of herbs to combine with water or oil to form a paste to rub into the skin.

**Ubtan**

¼ cup green mung beans
½ tsp cumin seeds
½ tsp turmeric powder for lighter skins
2 tsp turmeric powder for darker skins
a pinch of saffron powder
water or coconut oil to mix

Grind the mung beans and cumin seeds into a fine powder (using a coffee grinder), then blend with the turmeric and saffron powder. Store in a pot in the bathroom, along with a small bowl and spoon to mix into a paste.

Lightly exfoliate your skin with the ubtan before your shower then rinse with warm water.

Treat your face to a light coating of coconut oil then steam off the oil with a wet flannel. You may find that you don't need to moisturise afterwards.

If you have time, perform Abhyanga which is self body massage with warm oil. The type of oil is dependent on your Ayurvedic constitution, but almond or sesame are good for most people. Rub the oil onto your body starting at your feet with strokes towards your heart. This wakes up your circulation and helps your body eliminate toxins. Then wash off the excess oil in a hot bath or shower.

## Eating breakfast

Once dressed, we can take time to eat breakfast. This coconut rice is suited to all Ayurvedic constitutions. It's a warm breakfast that is soothing yet stimulating for the digestion.

**Coconut breakfast rice**
a handful of white basmati rice
equal parts water and coconut milk
a few cardamom pods
a few cloves
a pinch of salt

Pour the rice into a saucepan and add the liquid (the amount of liquid will vary so follow the instructions on your packet of rice). Add the spices and salt and allow to boil until it becomes creamy with a texture like rice pudding.

## Daytime

During the day, the sun is at its highest and this is the active time of the day - the time for making things happen. It's best to eat a good, nourishing meal at lunchtime.

The fire of the sun is the same fire that exists within us and by acknowledging this we can align our activities to be more in synch with the Earth's rhythm, and therefore we can work more efficiently.

# Evening

As the day comes to an end, it is natural that we feel the need to rest. As the moon rises and it becomes dark, our system slows down and we feel ready to sleep.

An evening routine is important in allowing us to get a restful sleep which in turn has an impact on the following day.

Enjoy dinner with a smile and focus on what you are eating. Then take some time to do something you enjoy, or spend time with loved ones. You can also perform Abhyanga (self body massage) at this time instead of the morning.

# Bedtime

Make yourself a comforting night time drink such as this spiced milk and sit quietly as you drink it before you fall asleep. Clove and cardamom are great for digestion and maintaining oral health. Turmeric is an anti-inflammatory and can keep coughs and colds at bay.

**Spiced almond milk**
1 cup of almond milk
a pinch of turmeric
1 tsp agave syrup
a couple of cardamom pods
a couple of cloves
a piece of cinnamon stick

Warm the milk with all the ingredients. Strain out the spices before drinking.

Read some light, positive passages from a book so you sleep with these thoughts resonating in your mind. Performing a warm sesame oil foot massage before bed is a great way to improve your health and get a restful night's sleep.

## Find your rhythm

By keeping this routine in your life, you give yourself time and space in the morning to connect to something higher. It gives you time to think and also the assurance that you are taking care of yourself. The effort required to put these things into place may initially be a bit of a struggle, but once you find your rhythm you will see that life opens up to many possibilities and there is in fact no separation between us and the world around us. This opens up an infinite space of possibility and incoming of knowledge and creative ideas that allow us to feel we are fulfilling our potential in life.

"BY KEEPING THIS ROUTINE IN YOUR LIFE, YOU GIVE YOURSELF TIME AND SPACE IN THE MORNING TO CONNECT TO SOMETHING HIGHER."

# SEASONS OF OURSELVES

*Words and photos by Ellie Beck*

Take inspiration from Mother Nature and allow
your own seasons to flow freely.

I often think of our lives as being made up of seasons, but not like the cyclic flow of the four seasons – something much more fluid. Spring does not always follow winter in the seasons of ourselves and there may not even be a clear cross over point when one ends and another begins. We may even have mini-seasons within seasons. When we are blooming in one area, something else might be budding or indeed dying.

My creative journey – making, writing and mindful noticing – continually encourages me to see that each day can fall under a different timescale or seasonal influence. And as someone who lives closely connected with nature and the whims of her fancies, I'm learning better every year to not fall victim of being annoyed that the rain didn't come, or that the rain in fact brought a gigantic storm. Instead, I try to find the space within each situation and discover the moments of joy, beauty, pain or inspiration – this is where we can learn to live with the erratic nature of being seasonal creatives.

My own seasons can change quickly based on my childrens' emotions each day. Children have a way of whirling through like a cyclone and ripping up our best creative moments, tearing into our captured stillness and whipping around our cups of tea.

There's a lot of talk about the balance of motherhood vs artist. I personally don't think there's a balance at all – often it's more of a big tangled mess. Like on a hot sweaty summer's day, whilst waiting for the relief of rain in an afternoon storm, but knowing it probably won't come. I would not give up any wintery storms to have only spring sunshine or autumn glory, because in my journey I am learning that without storms, the sunshine is not as bright. Without the dragging rain or battering of the ocean, there are not the insights into the fleeting sparkle on the sea, or the gentle quiet hand-holding while watching a new day's sunbeam.

I am a working textile artist and creative writer. I am also a full time stay-at-home mother. These two aspects of me need to

"DIVE DEEP INTO EACH SEASON AND DON'T BATTLE FOR WHAT HAS GONE."

fit side by side, or on top of each other. In my garden, the seasons come in starts and bursts – time and nature have a funny way of playing tricks on us. While one tree is in full bloom, another may be holding onto its buds tightly – not quite ready to give over to the next phase.

Over the years I've learnt to notice the moments when the creative summer is high and blossoming, and not feel sad when this coincides with a decay phase in another part of life. While one thing is glowing, it can be necessary to let another part of us fall aside like cast off golden leaves in autumn.

Just as the seasons of nature continually change, our lives are always shifting; nothing stays the same forever. Creative Self knows that soon this season of Other Self will flow into a new phase. And so, with this knowledge there comes an ease – a letting go, a joy in giving over to one season, not begrudging our full-time job, or our arduous moments of motherhood, or the depths of caring for a sick family member. At times it can be helpful to encourage our garden to succumb to one season without yearning for the new season to rush upon us. Give in, give over, allow, or gently lean into the season that may be stronger at that moment.

There is no fighting or holding tightly before the leaf swirls or the buds burst open. Right now we are in one particular season and soon life will swiftly move on again.

*Blue yarn dyed with indigo and pink with pokeweed (poisonous)*

# Ways to help our seasons flow

- Keep a journal or notebook of the creative ideas that flash through your mind while you're deep in a non-creative season.

- Give yourself fully to your work, your children and those other moments of life that demand you.

- Do not feel guilty taking time for your creative self. Make it a priority to factor in the seasons that you need to keep yourself growing, blooming and firmly rooted in the ground.

- Experiment and see which projects you can do in different seasons. You may find that aspects of your creative self actually flourish during what you once perceived as a winter season.

- Explain to your family, children, partner, or even colleagues how vital having Self time is.

- Dive deep into each season and don't battle for what has gone.

# ROOTED THROUGH TIME

*Words and photos by Alice Griffin*

"Just like the thousands of olive trees planted in Israel as a way to combat desertification, I could feel the olive tree rooting itself into my heart, showing me how to re-green my own journey and embark on a new path."

Looking out towards the Andalucian mountains my heart is aglow; orange, lemon and red hues dominate this desert landscape, but weaving it together are always the chain links of light, dark and shimmering green: The Olive. I feel my heart lift as I consider this tree's gnarled entwined trunks. I imagine its roots channelling up to six metres into the earth and marvel at its ability to withstand heat, drought, floods and even a little extreme cold. In awe of its resilience, adaptability and strength, I wrap my arms around my body holding tight and acknowledge that once again nature has taught me. As I prepare to leave this small Spanish village following a month of contemplation, I know I am

leaving with the answers I need and the olive-shaped word "rooted" firmly imprinted on my heart.

Known as the Tree of Eternity, the olive (*Olea europaea*) can live for thousands of years – and it has lived in my own heart forever. Unlike the predictable palm tree, it was the olive tree that held my attention during the dreary office days of my past. In my mind, the olive has always represented the perfect combination of exoticism and rustic practicality. I would daydream about time spent walking in hot, dusty landscapes with a backpack, pausing to rest under its branches to eat a sandwich, à la Laurie Lee. As time has moved on I have consistently been

# "I BELIEVE THAT NATURE PROVIDES US WITH SIGNS AND DELIVERS ANSWERS; WE JUST NEED TO TAKE NOTICE."

attracted to the olive, both as a symbol of far away places and for its stable longevity as a plant. It mirrors the dichotomy of my own life perfectly: itchy feet constantly in battle with a yearning for roots.

When I arrived in Spain at the beginning of the month, I came with questions: was it best for our family to continue with our itinerant lifestyle or was it the right time for us to stand still? These thoughts had been bubbling inside me throughout the past year and I knew I now had to face them – make decisions – and so the earth called to me once again. I believe that nature provides us with signs and delivers answers; we just need to take notice. Just as daffodils never fail to lift the heart as the first sign of spring, I believe the land can nourish

us in many ways – in spirit, beauty, medicinally, or by encouraging us to reflect. For me it was the arid landscape of Andalucia that I so longed for. It was this very place where my family and I spent almost six months ten years earlier – an experience that would propel us into what would become a decade of exploring, a life as wanderers, for which I am truly grateful. But now something has changed. Our love of living in narrow boats, campervans, cabins and cottages, all spread out across countries and time, is no longer weaving together neatly. Instead the fabric of our lifestyle is beginning to fray and in order to halt the unravelling we needed to make time to truly listen to our hearts, cut ourselves off. Reconnect. I knew there was no better place to do this than amidst the peacefulness of the Spanish mountains.

In the presence of such raw and seemingly impenetrable beauty and with the time to truly absorb, we began our journey towards brightness again. Surrounded as I was by olive trees I began to recognise that perhaps the problem was that my life had somehow become dried up and devoid of newness, so entrenched had I become in a sense of myself described in the obligatory bullet points of our generation. I was *Alice: traveller, wanderer, nomad, seeker of simple ways* – and yet the yearning I was feeling in my heart was for a house, for comfort and a solid place to root down in my home country. Suddenly I could feel the teachings, the energy feeding into me, and just like the thousands of olive trees planted in Israel *(Dr. Zohar Kerem, Faculty of Agriculture, Hebrew University, Jerusalem)* as a way to combat desertification, I could feel the olive tree rooting itself into my heart, showing me how to re-green my own journey and embark on a new path. The message weaving itself into my life's narrative – just as the crops being woven between rows in those Israeli olive tree forests – was that all elements of who we are can flourish together, and that sometimes the whole will be stronger for it.

The setting Spanish sun reflects on my face as I thank this evergreen tree – this symbol of life – for its wisdom, and consider its path through time: consistently resilient against all weathers in a rotation of blooming, fruiting and resting. I laugh with the knowledge of such a suddenly easy flow of answers and acknowledge that our lives, too, are a cycle; ups and downs, comings and goings, old and new. There's a combining of chapters that might often feel at odds with each other and yet in the end always come together to make a brilliant book. I realise that just like the olive, I can also be many things; loose like blossom yet rooted to my land, fruiting new adventures yet weathering the storm, and I know that I will be leaving Spain in search of my own English home and that the first tree I will plant there will be the olive so that I can be reminded of – and at peace with – the ever-evolving journey of life; of time. 🌿

# A TEA MEDITATION

## ...for experiencing herbs to the fullest.

Words by Marlene Adelmann & Jane Metzger
at the Herbal Academy.

* This article is excerpted and adapted from the Herbal Academy's online program, the *Herbal Materia Medica Course*. By studying plants one herb at a time, we have the opportunity to connect with individual herbs at a meaningful and in-depth level. For more information, visit: theherbalacademy.com/product/herbal-materia-medica-course

One of the easiest ways to experiment with herbs is to make tea. Herbalists create teas that can be soothing, uplifting, and supportive of healing. These can be made with just one herb or many. Choosing the right herbs is a learning process that requires the use not only of our herbal knowledge, but of our senses.

We inherently know to observe, touch, taste, and smell fresh or dried herbs, but listening is also part of the learning process when using plants. Sitting quietly with a plant, whether it is growing or dried, can help us tune in and turn off some of the outside chatter that may get in the way of learning some of the subtleties of each herb. Here are some practical tips for getting started, compiled into a simple tea meditation activity.

# The sense of taste

Our taste buds allow us to detect the flavours of foods and herbs both for enjoyment and for safety, but the act of tasting also initiates a physiological response. We can use our sense of taste to get a sense of the action an herb may have in our body.

Here are some ways you may describe tastes and what they mean *(Winston, 2010; Vickery, 2012):*

**Sweet** - found in carbohydrates like whole grains and herbs like liquorice or astragalus, sweet tastes are nourishing, building, and soothing.

**Salty** - found in mineral-rich foods and herbs like seaweed and nettle, salty tastes provide minerals, are building to bones, hair, and nails, and act as diuretics.

**Sour** - found in acid-rich sour foods and herbs such as citrus, blueberries, and sorrel, sour tastes astringe and tone tissues, check fluid loss, and stimulate digestion.

**Bitter** - found in plants such as coffee, dandelion, chamomile, and gentian, bitter herbs stimulate digestion and improve nutrient absorption and eliminatory processes.

**Pungent** - found in plants rich in volatile oils and allyl sulphides such as garlic, ginger, and mustard, pungent tastes are antimicrobial and stimulate circulation.

**Spicy** - found in plants rich in volatile oils and terpenes such as cayenne pepper, rosemary, and oregano, spicy tastes stimulate circulation, digestion, and the respiratory system and are antimicrobial.

**Acrid** - found in plants such as kava kava, black cohosh, and lobelia, acrid tastes are more of an irritating sensation in the mouth than a taste, and are often analgesic and antispasmodic.

**Astringent** - found in plants containing tannins such as black tea, raspberry leaf, and rose petal, astringent tastes are drying and toning to tissues and can help stop bleeding and diarrhoea.

**Bland/Slippery** - found in plants rich in mucilage such as marshmallow root, slippery elm bark, and flax seed, bland/slippery herbs are cooling and soothing to inflamed tissues and can have a laxative effect.

# Describing energetics by taste

A herb can be said to be warming or cooling, drying or moistening, constricting or relaxing, or have one of several other "energies" or physical characteristics that describe how it influences the body. Learning the energetics of a plant is interesting in itself, but it is also extremely practical when choosing herbs for a particular person.

Particular tastes are also often associated with particular energetics, so you can use your taste buds to help you interpret the energetics of a herb.

Here are four ways you may describe energetics, and tastes that are often associated with them:

**Warming** - sweet, most pungent, and some spicy herbs are warming.

**Cooling** - sour, salty, bland, and bitter herbs are typically cooling.

**Drying** - sour, salty, spicy, bitter, and astringent herbs are typically drying.

**Moistening** - sweet and slippery herbs are typically moistening.

58

You may notice an emotional quality of a herb when you tune in to its energy. Some of these descriptions may include the sense that a herb is grounding, calming, gentle, centering, uplifting, energizing, expansive, nourishing, sensual, playful, loving, protective, opening, wise, kind, motherly, focusing or joyful, to name a few.

Now that you are familiar with the tastes and energetics of herbs, it's time to experience and observe your herb first hand via a simple tea meditation...

# Try the tea meditation exercise

You can experience the taste of a herb as an unsweetened tea and then read about the herb in herbal books to see if your impressions match the taste and energetics described by others. You might consider doing a tea meditation prior to researching the taste and energetics of your herb so you aren't influenced by what you've read! That being said, there is something to learn from each interaction with a plant, even one that is very familiar to you. It's just a matter of tuning in.

Conducting a tea meditation is a lovely and effective way to experience the properties of a plant and connect with it on a deeper level. Don't worry, you don't have to be experienced at meditation or consider yourself particularly intuitive—your physical senses and observational skills and a genuine desire to connect with the plant are really all that you need. We all have the ability to access this knowledge.

Through this simple tea meditation we can engage with the herbs we are using on a deeper level. We are able to slow down, listen to our bodies, and feel the energies and effects of the herbs. We may move out of our practice with new insights, a sense of well being, and renewed energy for all the wonderful learning ahead!

*Photography within entire article by Herbal Academy*

## Let's begin

1. Brew a cup of tea using just one plant (no blends). While it is infusing or decocting, grab a journal and a pen.

2. Find a quiet spot—this can be anywhere—your kitchen table, your couch, on a cushion on the floor, or outside under a tree.

3. Find a comfy seated position.

4. Close your eyes and take a deep, clearing breath. Smell the fragrant steam rising from your tea. What scents do you smell? How does the fragrant steam make your sinus passages or other parts of your body feel? Spend a few moments just breathing with the tea.

5. Take a sip and notice the taste in your mouth. Is it sweet, salty, pungent, sour, bitter? Is it astringent (drying) or slippery (moistening)? What other tastes do you notice? Earthy, swampy, floral?

6. Continue to sip and notice how the tea makes you feel. Is it warming or cooling? Drying or moistening? Where do you feel it in your body? This is often just taking note of where in your body your attention is drawn. For example, ginger will likely feel warming and you may notice it in your stomach. This will give you a clue to one of its actions as a digestive. Rooty herbs like burdock or American ginseng are often grounding, making your tailbone feel rooted to the spot in which you are sitting.

7. Does the plant have a personality that comes through to you? Do you experience it as a male energy or female energy? Does it feel like a light, happy, laughing child or a sombre, wise elder? This is a representation of the plant's energy.

8. You might ask the plant if it offers any particular support for you, and then notice if your awareness settles on any particular part of your body. This may be subtle, or the plant may communicate with you strongly. You may not notice anything, and that's okay too.

9. Come out of your reverie slowly, and take a moment to note any observations in your journal. This will become a valuable record of your interactions with individual plants, and help you build your knowledge of and connection with them. 🌿

### References

VICKERY, N. (2012). *Re-engaging our senses: Taste.* Blog article. Accessed online May 2018: www.thefamilyherbalist.wordpress.com/2012/09/07/re-engaging-our-senses-taste

WINSTON, D. (2010). *The ten tastes.* Video. Center for Herbal Studies (www.herbalstudies.net). Accessed online May 2018: www.youtube.com/watch?v=FosnZVlFGPA

# THE
# PERFECT
# LOAF

Tara Rose talks to Maurizio Leo about the art of
sourdough baking and how *time* is a crucial ingredient.
Bread also brings back memories for many of us.
*"Good food can instantly link us back to a time in our past—
almost like reliving the moment."*

*Interview by Tara Rose*
*Photos by Maurizio Leo*

**How did you learn to bake sourdough bread?**

Years ago, I was given a gift - a book on how to bake sourdough bread at home. As I casually started reading the book, I slowly felt myself falling deeper and deeper into the process of it all. I read the book several times and finally began experimenting with creating my first sourdough starter - which was not immediately easy.

But the marrying of science and craft overtook me, and after a few tries adjusting flour, temperature and every other parameter, I finally had my first starter up and running.

When I pulled my first sourdough boule from the oven, I was astonished at the transformation that had taken place over the course of just two days: from seemingly lifeless flour and water to an incredible-tasting loaf, teeming with energy and flavour. From that very first loaf, I was hooked. Now I bake almost every day at home.

My learning and discovery has come primarily from reading books, trial and error, and my attempts to understand the underlying process.

**Some bakers claim that their sourdough starter is decades old. Can you explain how that might be possible?**

With proper conditions and maintenance a sourdough starter could in theory continue to live indefinitely. As long as fresh food (flour and water) are provided, and the temperature range in which it is kept is not drastically changed, it should be happy and continue to do the job of fermentation for many, many years.

I've talked to bakers who have had their starter for more than 40 years and it's just as vigorous as the day it was created. I've also talked to other bakers who actually prefer to create a new one each year, as a blank slate with a young, vibrant starter. Either way, these resilient mixtures of bubbling life are happy to help us leaven and flavour dough into delicious bread.

# "AS EACH STEP PROGRESSES, I STEP BACK AND ASSESS THE DOUGH – DOES IT NEED MORE TIME?"

**It's often said that love is the secret ingredient? When it comes to baking good bread, would you agree that time is really the most important factor?**

Time is a critical component to making great bread and you'll often hear the saying *"real bread can't be rushed"*, which holds true. Sure, there are parameters you can adjust to speed up the process slightly, but take it too far and you'll compromise taste and texture.

Naturally leavened bread takes time to achieve full fermentation. If it's rushed you could end up with a bread that simply isn't as appealing as it would have been, given enough time for the yeast and bacteria in your sourdough starter to fully metabolise and work through the dough.

One of the most important things I learned when I first started baking

was to always be willing to adjust my schedule in response to how the dough is developing. I start my day baking with a loose timeline: build my levain in the morning, give it several hours to ripen, mix the dough and begin bulk fermentation, and so forth. As each step progresses, I step back and assess the dough - does it need more time?

**All good bread starts with good grain. Can you share some of your favourite varieties?**

You only need three ingredients to make great bread: flour, water, and salt. Because there are only three ingredients, each one plays a vital role in the end product. Bread doesn't start with the baker, it starts with the farmers caring for their soil and growing the grain. The more we can do to support local farmers and growers, the more we ensure our grain is of the highest quality.

Spelt is one of my favourites. It has a nutty sweetness that permeates the entire loaf, even more so when it's freshly milled. And khorasan, which has a beautiful golden colour, high protein content for added nutrition, and a sweet, buttery flavour.

**What recommendations do you have for those who would like to venture into the world of sourdough at home?**

My first suggestion is to drop any preconceived notions about the difficulty of baking sourdough at home. It can be as involved or as simple as you like!

Gather a few tools to make the job easier (such as scales) and get in and get your hands dirty. The best way to learn to bake bread is to bake bread. Next, find a good starting recipe and stick to that recipe for a while. It's easy to get lost in the variables with baking but if you stick to the same formula for several bakes, it's easier to connect the dots and draw conclusions when the baking environment changes.

**Do you see bread baking as a creative act? Can you share your process with us? I would love to know what inspires you.**

Definitely! Bread is made by a baker's own hands. The baker is the one who imparts their unique style to it.

Looking at what other bakers are making, whether at home or in a professional bakery, always has my mind spinning with inspiration for new processes, grains and experiments to try.

I develop my recipes by drawing on ingredients and food that have meaning to me. This might be from a family meal I've had in the past or from a flavour combination I've been dreaming of and testing in my kitchen.

I like to first focus on the base of flavour I want to work with. If I'm looking to add fruits, nuts, or other spices, I like to see how the mix-ins can further balance or heighten the flavours without complicating or muddling the flavour profile. Sometimes it takes me several tries to get the formula just right. It's this constant tinkering and testing that adds

even more meaning to the final loaf as it emerges from the oven.

**Are you, in your own way, re-inventing the sourdough?**

Bread has been baked throughout human history and I don't feel like my approach is vastly different from anyone else's. However, in a way we're all trying to discover our unique take on baking bread - whether it's at home or professionally in a bakery. One of the most fascinating things about bread is that you can have two different bakers bake the exact same formula and end up with two completely different loaves. In a way, we're all creating bread that's unique each time we bake.

**I believe the perfect loaf is not an elusive thing for you. Yet, has there been a time, when all the components came together in such profound alchemy that you said to yourself, not so quietly, *"I am a genius"*?**

I named my baking website *The Perfect Loaf* because it was about my journey in discovering the "perfect" bread I had constructed in my mind so long ago. This lofty goal is always changing with each bread I bake. My website has become an ongoing journal of my baking trials and experiments to share what I've learned along the way.

Honestly, I don't feel like I'll ever create the perfect loaf. I think most bakers have an idea of what that loaf would look like, what it would feel like, even taste like, but it might be an end goal that'll never be reached. It's what keeps us baking and pushing.

I can look back at the bakes I've done over the years and definitely see remarkable improvements. We're always evolving as bakers - and that's the exciting part.

**What should one be looking for when buying good bread?**

I first look for sufficient crust colour. The outside of the loaf should be well-coloured, with colours that range from light brown to dark mahogany. Quite a lot can be gleaned from how the bread was prepared just by looking at the crust. Next, ask if you can sample a piece of the bread for sale. The interior should show signs of proper fermentation: no dense spots or raw flour, it should be well aerated. I look for a flavour that's not too sour but still has plenty of complexity and depth (although this is a very subjective thing). Each bite should have a pleasing mouthfeel and not be stiff or rough. In the end "good bread" is ultimately decided upon by the buyer!

**How do you store your loaves?**

This very much depends on your climate and location. I have a few recommendations no matter where you live: first, cut your loaf directly in half. Start cutting slices from the inside outand when done, turn the inside of the loaf down on the cutting board. This way the interior is not exposed to air. It's protected by the crust and the cutting board. After a few days I transfer my loaf to a bread box - a very valuable item in my kitchen. This helps hold in just enough moisture without the bread becoming too soft. It does not need to be stored in the refrigerator.

**Bread, to me, could be the ultimate Proustian experience. What are your thoughts on that?**

An expertly crafted loaf with a dark and crunchy crust, tender interior, and deep flavour complexity... Bread can absolutely bring forth a memorable time in one's past. Even if it's not specifically the bread you're recalling, perhaps it's an event or moment in time when you were gathered around the dinner table with family, or eating sandwiches at your favourite hidden beach spot.

Good food can instantly link us back to a time in our past—almost like reliving the moment.

*Visit theperfectloaf.com for Maurizio's sourdough recipes and blog.*

"GOOD FOOD CAN INSTANTLY LINK US BACK TO A TIME IN OUR PAST– ALMOST LIKE RELIVING THE MOMENT."

# WILD FERMENTING

*Recipes and photos by Eleonora Matarrese*

Fermented foods are good for both our body and soul. You
are probably familiar with sauerkraut (fermented cabbage)
but it's just as easy to ferment other vegetables at home. Here
are three recipes, which all work together deliciously in a wild
salad. Use these suggestions as a starting point and adapt them
depending on what is in season for you right now.

Buon appetito!

# fermented carrots

## What you need

- **Fresh vegetables** of your choice - we'll use carrots here.
- **1 litre water**: don't use tap water as it contains chlorine. Either use bottled water or leave a bowl of tap water overnight so the chlorine evaporates.
- **2 tbsp sea salt,** or better yet, use 1 litre sea water (which naturally contains salt).
- **Glass jar** (sterilised)
- **Cloth & elastic band**

## Method

1. Rinse your carrots to remove any residual soil. Leave the skin on and slice them into strips.

2. Place the slices of carrot in the sterilised glass jar leaving a little space at the top - as wide as a finger.

3. In a bowl, prepare the brine: add 2 tbsp salt into 1 litre water and stir to dissolve. (Technically, we should use 2% salt in the winter when it is colder and fermentation is slower and 7% in summer).

4. Pour the brine onto your carrots.

5. Decide if you'd like to add any herbs as flavouring, such as garlic mustard (*Alliaria petiolata*) leaves and flowers, wild garlic (*Allium ursinum* - you can use all parts of the plant!), cumin seeds (*Carum carvi*), wild fennel (*Fœniculum vulgare*), or angelica (*Angelica archangelica*). If you use leafy herbs, it's best to use the woody twigs that are left after removing leaves, as the leaves themselves could become too soft. It's a way to recycle twigs after you have used the leaves for cooking!

6. Once you've added your flavouring, close the jar and shake.

7. Remove the lid and cover the jar with a cloth and rubber band. Leave the jar on the kitchen counter away from heat sources.

8. Allow the jar to stand for three days. A white foam may form: this is yeast. You can remove it and throw it into the compost or use it instead of baking powder. Vegetables must always remain under the liquid. If they develop mould then something has gone wrong and for safety you will have to throw everything away, but it almost never happens. Of course during the preparation, ensure that all the tools are clean, as well as your hands.

9. From the morning of the third day, start to taste: when the taste is to your liking, close the lid and place in the fridge. Fermented food lasts a very long time, but I'm pretty sure it won't remain uneaten for long!

# Verjus "green juice"

The name *verjus* comes from middle French – "vert" and "jus" which means "green juice". It is a highly acidic juice you can make by pressing unripe grapes, apples or other sour fruit, or even from wild herbs, for example extracting juice from wood sorrel *(Oxalis acetosella)* or sorrel *(Rumex spp.)*. You can also add other herbs and spices to enhance its flavour, such as chive stalks *(Allium schœnoprasum)* or chopped wild garlic *(Allium ursinum)*. It's delicious when drizzled over salads in the place of vinegar.

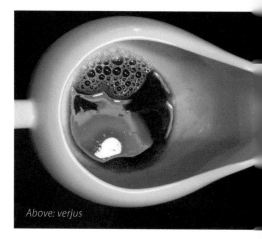
*Above: verjus*

Simply put your juice of choice in a glass or bottle and let it ferment for 24 hours. It'll soon be ready for use or you can preserve it (with the bottle closed, of course) in your fridge. If you'd like your verjus to be clear, you can strain it and add lemon juice. You don't need to do this for sorrel or wood sorrel juice since they already contain citric acid.

In the Middle Ages verjus was widely used instead of vinegar or lemon juice - particularly in Nordic countries where lemons and grapes didn't grow. In Syria it is called *husroum* and today it is still made by female members of land-owning clans: it will be distributed within the extended family and used throughout the year. What is amazing about verjus is that it doesn't alter other flavours in the same way that vinegar and lemon juice do.

# fermented syrup

This fermented syrup is an ancient recipe. You can potentially use any herb, but in Italy it is mainly prepared with fir* sprouts or pine* buds or cones or with mint *(Menta spp.)* or lemon balm *(Melissa officinalis)*.

Put your leaves, seeds or buds a glass jar and cover them with sugar (or honey), using the same amount of plants as sugar. Then close the jar and place in the sun. The sun's warmth melts the sugar and this ferments the leaves to produce a pure syrup – rich, nutritious and with a concentrated flavour. The great-grandmothers in Puglia, southern Italy, say a jar needs *"forty days of clear sunshine"* to ferment. Drizzle the syrup on yogurt or ice cream, use it to make sauces, or diluted for an infusion.

*\* Fir and pine should not be consumed by pregnant or breastfeeding women, or children under the age of three.*

# Wild salad

## Ingredients

- Use a mixture of dandelion leaves (*Taraxacum officinale*), wild garlic leaves and buds (*Allium ursinum*), violet flowers (*Viola odorata*), daisies (*Bellis perennis*), and any other greens of your choice.

- Fermented carrots.

- Fermented syrup made with wild fennel seeds (*Fœniculum vulgare*).

- Verjus made with alexanders leaves (*Smyrnium olusatrum*).

## Method

1. In a bowl put your greens – clean and chopped as you like.

2. Add in the fermented carrots.

3. Season with a vinaigrette made with your fennel seed syrup and alexanders verjus. (You don't need any salt.) Enjoy!

*- For more recipes, see Eleonora Matarrese's new book: 'La Cuoca Selvatica - Storie e Ricette per portare la Natura in Tavola'.*

# STAY WILD

*Interview by Tara Rose*

Tara Rose talks to Raphaëlle Gagnon of Boreal Folk Apothecary. Raphaëlle and her partner Mark adventure across Canada in their 1967 bus handcrafting natural skincare goods made from wild botanicals.

**The way you live and work is very evocative of a sense of embracing the wild side that is innate in all of us. We seem to have forgotten it and many of us are wanting to get in touch with it again. Can we talk more about this?**

From my experience so far in life, I feel that there are two predominant wild sides to people. One wild side is being in tune with our natural environment and *animalistic-self* whilst minding a close connection to the earth. The other is being a *non-conforming soul*, seeking freedom and happiness by following one's heart's desires and dreams, regardless of the risks involved in treading uncertain waters. I believe I fall somewhere in between these two types of wild.

I grew up in a French Canadian family of rather wild folk. They were bushmen – loggers, hunters, fishermen and farmers. As a young girl, my grandfather would tell me stories of walking in the bush for 4 to 5 months at a time. He would leave with nothing more than a rucksack, an axe, and a bag of flour and sugar. My father would later recount his hitchhiking odysseys across North America during the '70s.

Those stories always ignited some kind of fire in me. *Freedom Fighters* is what my father would call people protecting the wilderness and inner wildness. I am proud to come from a family whose roots are deeply intertwined with the wilderness.

Ever since I can remember, I've had this deep yearning for nature and freedom. Growing up, every time I spent time working in nature, camping or canoeing, something in me would come alive; in fact it would roar and scream. It was a feeling of connectedness, a feeling of unquestionable belonging. I knew at a young age that I wanted to live a free life alongside nature. I knew I was a person led by curiosity, travel, and adventure, with a strong creative side. So, at the age of 14, I decided to live an unconventional life.

I believe we all have this wild blood running through our veins. The only thing separating us from living a more wild life – whether internal or external – is the decision to do so. I feel deeply thankful to have met a life partner who is also a free spirit and honours our choice to live wildly and freely.

**Time is perhaps the most precious factor in our lives today. How do you experience and allow time in the process of making your products?**

Photo by kellybrownphotographer.com

My time is dictated by the seasons and its gifts. The rest simply flows.

Winter is a time of introspection for ourselves and Boreal Folk. We take the time to formulate new products, experiment with new recipes, and work on the computer and business side of things.

In the spring, we slowly begin our harvests with the appearance of nettles, spruce tips and poplar buds around us. This cyclical routine allows us to nourish ourselves with wild greens too, as we begin distilling, infusing and extracting our harvests.

Summer is our busiest time of the year as we travel throughout western Canada harvesting fireweed, wild roses, horsetail, mint, juniper berries, labrador tea and wild sage, to name a few. It is a dance we perform to find balance between formulating the products, and harvesting and vending at festivals and farmers' markets.

As plants begin returning to the earth in the fall, we continue harvesting by distilling fir, spruce and sweet gale. We conclude the year by picking mushrooms and autumn fruits such as huckleberries and rosehips.

It is important to mention that we do feel the need to park our wilderness lab for a few weeks uninterrupted by travel each season in order to produce our goods. These are my favourite moments and when I feel most of the magic happens. Nestled somewhere in the wilderness, brewing up our potions to the sound of the swaying pine trees, the

wild horses grazing around us, all in the midst of wild botanical abundance.

**You wildcraft some of the most amazing botanical treasures on the planet. Can you talk about some of your absolute favourites that are also unique to where you are located?**

I am deeply inspired by my immediate surroundings. Unlike many skincare formulators, I do not seek after luxurious oils, butters and scents from across the globe. What inspires me and makes our products unique is that we try to stay as local as possible to Canada. My partner and I harvest unique plants that we choose for their skin care properties.

We also source 230 million-year-old salt and clay. These ingredients are from an ancient ocean which left a mineral-rich deposit hundreds of metres beneath the prairies. Our bath soaks, made with these Canadian salt crystals, smell and feel absolutely divine. It is like bathing in a pristine, ancient growth forest.

"MY TIME IS DICTATED BY THE SEASONS AND ITS GIFTS. THE REST SIMPLY FLOWS."

One of my favourite harvests is the fireweed harvest. I spent many years planting trees in disturbed soils and this tall purple flowering plant would always keep me close company. In the early spring, I pick its shoots when they are only a few inches tall. It is known at that stage as wild asparagus because of the similarity in taste. Later in the summer, we harvest the flowers and leaves. This plant helps to reduce inflammation of the skin and is valued for its nourishing and soothing virtues.

Another unique pick in our region is the spring harvest of balsam poplar buds. This gooey and uniquely scented harvest is prized for its pain relieving properties. The high salicin content of the buds helps to relieve muscular discomforts and skin irritation. The unique scent of poplar buds smells of warm honey on a spring day. I am absolutely captivated by it.

**How do the seasons and the cycles of growth affect the way you view the land and your materials when you make your beautiful products?**

All of Canada has become our backyard over the years. I feel blessed to travel its nooks and crannies and call many different places home. I'm always humbled at how ephemeral each harvest window is. Take the wild rose season — what an intoxicating tease! It only lasts a couple of weeks, if that. Each moment is fleeting within nature and it makes me appreciative to witness and be part of its natural cycles.

In a way, I feel like I am a guardian of time.

# "ALL OF CANADA HAS BECOME OUR BACKYARD OVER THE YEARS."

As you walk into our wilderness lab and start opening up jars of dried plants and infused oils, memories of early spring or a mid-summer eve will surely be evoked.

As we travel throughout the land in our 50-year-old bus, the seasons change as our environment perpetually does as well. When we retreat into the bush, we choose areas that are legal to park and harvest in. Most often, it's our first time exploring these areas, so the harvest depends on my calculated guesses. I look at maps to see which kind of terrain are in the region and guess which plants will grow there. Often, we are pleasantly surprised and at other times, quietly disappointed.

It is unique to have a business which depends on the finding of wild plants. Every year, the growing season is different. Perhaps there was an abundance of wild mint this year but next year we will seldom find any. Last spring, the growing season was over a month late. It teaches one to be observant, patient and receptive. Our products are dependent on these harvests, but they can also be adapted at any time.

"I WILL NEVER KNOW EVERYTHING THAT THE PLANT WORLD HAS TO TEACH, WHICH IS WHY I LOVE IT SO MUCH. I WILL FOREVER REMAIN A STUDENT."

Photo by Mackenzie Duncan - themackenzielife.com

I thank the mountains, streams, bogs and valleys for their abundance and pristine existence.

**You have planted more than 2.3 million trees in northern Canada. How did you get into such a brave and bold project and what is the impact of such an action on the future of our ecology?**

Do you remember earlier when I mentioned my wild inner longing to live in freedom from a young age? Well, following that inner call, at 19 years old, after my second year of university, I jumped on a plane and flew 5000 kilometres to a place I had never been before. Beautiful British Columbia.

I didn't know a single soul out West. I had been hired through the Internet to plant trees for a summer. I brought a shovel, my tent, some mountaineering boots and a mentality to conquer one of the toughest jobs on the planet.

Spending my days alone with thousands of seedlings to plant, I quickly fell in love with the wildness of the work. Gruesome and raw, with hands in the dirt. For a decade, I would spend each summer planting hundreds of thousands of trees in the northern Boreal forest. We'd build remote bush camps where a helicopter would drop us off because there were no roads. We would not leave that camp until all the millions of trees for that area were planted. Sometimes we would be in the bush a month and a half before getting a 30-minute helicopter ride to the nearest town of 2000 people.

We never knew what day of the week it was. Dirt was perpetually lodged under our fingernails and our skin turned to leather from living and working in clear cuts. This is where my love for the Boreal forest unfolded itself. I became enamoured with the small scraggly spruce and tamarack trees that grow in the bogs; the crunchy lichen that lives on top of sandy dunes; its defensive sand cranes and curious black bears. I loved the loud songs that the swamp creatures would sing at night and the sweet smell of pine needles roasting in the sun on a hot summer day.

I planted 2.3 million trees, most of which were spruce, with my own two hands. I spent thousands of hours alone dreaming up my future in the silence of the northern Boreal forest. Many of the trees I planted will be harvested for the next generation's needs. Although, I'm hoping that perhaps by then we'll have found more sustainable ways to produce and harvest lumber.

**As time passes and your learning deepens and expands in so many ways, how do you feel and what do you notice about your close and daily interactions with the plant world and the way the wilderness is affecting you?**

Working with the plant world is infinite work. I will never know everything that the plant world has to teach, which is why I love it so much. I will forever remain a student. The botanical world is so complex that it can nourish my growth as I evolve. The wilderness is my greatest teacher and the most potent medicine. 🖋

*To find out more, visit: borealfolk.ca*

"Weeds are flowers too,
once you get to know them."

— A.A. Milne

Clockwise from top left: *Epilobium hirsutum, Ranunculus acris friesianus,*
*Centaurea scabiosa, Papaver rhoeas*

# THE MEADOW'S EDGE

*Words and photos by Lindsay Buck*

A story about discovering a new land through its
wildflowers, plus tips on how to start a *Herbarium* —
a catalogue of pressed plants.

With the thick black mud tugging gently
on my Wellingtons, I trace the well-
worn path along the meadow's edge
where the grasses bow low from the
footprints of many evening strolls. The
snow is still clinging to the mountain
peaks in the distance, but in these rolling
foothills the white winter blanket has
been pulled back to reveal an electric
green–the colour of the Swiss meadow
in Spring. Seemingly overnight, swaths
of minute purple speedwells, delicate-
petalled anemones and sweet-scented
violets have painted the hillsides with
their colour and now lend their crispness
to the cool air. Not so long ago, these
beloved meadows were completely
unknown to me.

I can recall my first walks in these
meadows. They were uneasy and
strained. The mud didn't tug; it pulled
naggingly at my boots. The air wasn't

crisp; it was cutting. Time–I suddenly
seemed to have so much of it. New to
Switzerland, I was struggling to embrace
the newfound luxury of a slow lifestyle
against the backdrop of my previously
bustling life. What was I missing out on
while standing here, literally stuck in the
mud? For the past decade, professional
successes had been measured solely
by long hours logged in meetings or in
front of a screen. With this false façade
wearing away, I felt exposed. But nature,
as it so often does, offered exactly the
comfort I needed to help reconcile the
distant past, my recent past, and my
future here in a new place.

Spring–it brings that feeling of hope
and renewal with an intensity that is
somehow surprising every year. Those
first early rays of sunshine pulled up
bouquets of wildflower blooms, and
with them, my rooted childhood

memories. This is why I became a landscape architect in the first place, I remembered–my love for plants, my awe and respect for nature, and an undying belief in the importance of people connecting to their environment. I saw these meadows with new eyes. I became fascinated with the diversity of plant life, both brilliant and diminutive, that I was encountering on a daily basis and wanted to put names to what I was finding. I felt called to test my own beliefs by becoming intimate with my new surroundings.

It started casually enough, with a few wildflowers plucked from the masses, pressed lovingly between pages of books, to be identified and then tucked into my knowledge bank at a later date. But the dabbling affair quickly became so much more: a scientific exploration, and artistic endeavour, and in the end, a lifestyle – the way I now observe my life in relation to time and nature throughout the seasons.

Keeping a herbarium resets your life's clock. Hurriedly running between destinations loses its appeal when a leisurely stroll is so much more fruitful. Who knew the plant riches held between sidewalk cracks or tucked amongst the fence posts? With eyes attuned to wildflowers, the days no longer run together, but become broken up into what's about to bloom or what is now blossoming that wasn't before, sometimes down to the hour. Watchers of plants unwittingly begin to notice other things in the environment: *Mullein growing here? The soil in this area must be dry. Are the poppy blossoms curled up?*

Rain must be on the way. Seasonal shifts become both more apparent and incremental as the blossoms on your usual route slowly turn to seed and concede to the next buds that are about to burst.

Working with the plants teaches patience–arranging them just right on the flower press, resisting the temptation to peek while they take their time to dry. Mounting the dried specimens is meditative–applying adhesive means carefully tracing the outline of their structure with the brush, feeling and for the first time noting the different texture and form of each species. The science of identifying the plant and cataloguing its details gives way to the celebration of the unique beauty in each plant: art.

With a current herbarium collection approaching 400 different species, I have come out on the other side transformed, with a true sense of fulfilment. While my days and weeks are still filled with the bustle of career and family life, the time I now set aside to spend learning about my surroundings are the truly enjoyable hours of the day. This is what has given me a renewed sense of inspiration towards my profession as a landscape architect. Researching each plant and learning about its uses–how it connects people to their surroundings–has rekindled my passion for nature and returned my sense of wonder that first inspired me as a child.

PLANTS ARE MAGIC #3 TIME

# tips for starting your own herbarium

## Collecting

- Look along pathways, field/woodland borders and fence lines. Edges have the most diversity!
- Be aware of restrictions: never collect from nature reserves and be knowledgeable of species that are protected in your area.
- Collect all parts of the plant that can help in identification, including flowers, seed pods, and basal leaves. Often, a single bloom and leaf from each plant is sufficient, leaving the remainder of the plant alive and intact.
- Don't forget to note the details: recording the date of collection is a potential identification tool. And as a bonus, this helps track how bloom times differ from year to year for each species.

## Pressing

- Heavy books work in a pinch, but a simple plant press allows the pressure to be more carefully applied and adjusted.
- Arrange plants to minimize overlapping parts.
- Parchment paper above and below the plants helps retain the colour on delicate specimens, which newspaper might otherwise pull away.
- Most plants need between one and two weeks to be fully dried.

## Mounting + Storing

- Use acid-free paper and lightfast, age-resistant glue to ensure preservation of the specimens.
- Touch the dried plants as little as possible as oils from the skin can damage them. Work with tweezers to move the plants and hold them down.
- Work quickly but carefully, applying adhesive to delicate petals last to avoid curling from dried glue.
- Freeze mounted specimens for 72 hours to eliminate any harmful insects or fungus.
- Store final specimens away from direct sunlight to prevent light damage and fading.

*To see step-by-step herbarium instructions and an online catalogue*
*of finished specimens, visit www.freshlypressed.ch*

# GOLDENROD

Words and photos by Ginny Farquhar

## "I FELT DYEING RUNNING DEEP IN MY ANCESTRAL VEINS."

Two years ago, my parents moved to a flat and sadly said goodbye to the beautiful garden that they had nurtured since 1962. They dug up a goldenrod plant and gave it to me in a pot - the same plant that had originally come from my grandfather's garden decades earlier.

My mother and I share a special connection with goldenrod as we have both used it to dye fibre.

Goldenrod (*Solidago*) is a perennial from the aster family. In late summer, spires of tiny yellow florets open; happy yellow blooms which are adored by nectar-seeking insects.

When I was a child, my mother explored plant dyeing and I recall watching her use large wooden tongs to add skeins of yarn to pots of gently simmering liquids on the kitchen stove. She kept meticulous notes of her experiments which I am now fortunate to possess.

On referring to her records I discovered that she dyed yarn with her garden goldenrod on 1 September 1975. Last year, I thought it would be wonderful to use the very same plant on the same day. I cropped some flowers, soaked them overnight, then I used heat to extract the dye colour and strained off the golden liquid. Using her plant was joyous, knowing that the process I was slowly working through was almost the same as hers 42 years previously.

Moving the fabric in the dye bath brought about a deep and unexplainable peace - a reverence and complete connection to my mother. In those moments, I felt dyeing running deep in my ancestral veins. My craving to use plants to colour cloth in this slow and sustainable way was continuing a tradition. I stitched her a small heart with the fabric I had dyed and filled it with dried goldenrod flowers. It is imbued with connection, family history and love. 🌿

1 September 1975

---

Goldenrod Dye Recipe

2 oz goldenrod flowers
2 pints water

1. Remove flower heads
   from plant - no leaves!
2. Boil, then simmer for 30
   minutes.
3. Remove flowers then add
   fibre.
4. Simmer for 30 minutes.
5. Cool in dye bath.

# MEMORY IN CLOTH

*Words & tutorial by Samorn Sanixay*
*Photos by Lorna Sim (Canberra, Australia)*

Keep a lasting memory of flowers by transferring them onto fabric with this flower pounding method. Try this when you have some beautiful flowers, but not enough to extract colour in your dye pot. The next best thing is to preserve them intact - in a print - just as you see them.

## What you need

Two pieces of thick cotton or linen fabric

Medium size mallet or hammer

Large wooden board/cardboard placed underneath fabric. Never place fabric directly on concrete as you will create holes in the fabric.

## Choosing plants

It is best to use darker coloured flowers and leaves with strong pigment. To check for pigment in flowers, rub a petal between your fingertips to see if the colour stains. If there is no staining on your fingers, there will be no colour transfer onto the cloth. In general the colour from yellow flowers will fade away.

You can try any flower or leaf that is growing in your garden or neighbourhood. Experiment with your local flora to see what works for you, but these are some suggestions.

**Leaves**: rose, maple, tomato, ferns, parsley, sage, young oak.

**Flowers**: rose, dahlia, geranium, marigold, snap dragon, poppy.

## Preparing your fabric

Prewash your fabric to remove any residual oils. Old fabric works well as it's likely been washed many times in the past.

Then soak your fabric in a bucket of ¼ vinegar and ¾ water solution. Leave to soak for 30 minutes then remove and allow to dry.

As an alternative to vinegar, pretreat with diluted soya milk as per the instructions in *Botanical Colour at your Fingertips* (2016) by Rebecca Desnos.

## Pounding the plants into fabric

1. Place the fabric onto the wooden board, then add the leaves and petals to the fabric.

2. Cover the fabric with another piece of cotton so that when you pound the leaves it will protect your work.

3. Pound each leaf under the cotton to reveal the print.

4. Keep going until you have created your desired pattern. You will have prints on both pieces of fabric.

5. Leave to dry for at least 24 hours.

6. Shake to remove dried petals, then iron to seal the dye and colour.

## Why do we need to cover when pounding?

If you pound the flowers without a cover, bits will go flying and splatter all over the place and create a mess instead of producing a crisp print of each flower or leaf. It's a bit like cooking food without a lid. The layer of fabric keeps everything contained and protects your work.

## How well do the colours last after washing?

With this technique, some colours from flowers will fade, but many leaf prints will retain their colour even after repeated washes. The darkest pigments usually indicate that colours will last the longest.

Flower pounding is best used for decorative items such as cushion covers or bags that don't require frequent washing.

Before starting a project, do a small test on a spare piece of fabric to see if the dye from the plant transfers onto fabric. Then wash the sample a couple of times to check that it has staying power. The dye in many leaves is substantive and immediately permanent. Use the plant guide on the previous pages as a starting point and then experiment with your local flora. 🌿

# PAPER MAKING

*Words and photos by Desiree Bell*

Making paper is a rewarding experience when you embed seeds, leaves, grasses or flowers (fresh or dried) that you have grown, collected or pressed, giving your paper a personal touch of colour and texture. Follow these step-by-step instructions to make your own recycled botanical paper.

## Equipment you need

1. Mold (a frame with a screen)

2. Deckle (an open frame)

3. Dishpan or container to hold water

4. Blender for creating pulp

5. Pieces of felt to extract water

6. Rolling pin to remove water

7. Sponge to soak up water

## Materials

- Old paper such as envelopes, drawing paper, construction paper, wrapping paper or paper bags. Do not use paper with black print, as it will turn the paper grey, and do not use glossy paper.

- Dried botanicals to embed into paper.

# Let's make some botanical paper

*Have fun and be prepared to get wet!*

1. Tear the paper into 1 or 2 inch pieces or use an office shredder.

2. Put 1 cup of paper into the blender and add 4 cups of warm water. Blend for 15 to 30 seconds until the paper becomes loose pulp. Pour the pulp into the container. Repeat this step until you have 2 inches of pulp in your container.

3. Botanicals can be added to the blender or container. Soak botanicals in water before using to lessen the fading or bleeding.

4. Mix the water with your hands to distribute the fibre and botanicals evenly throughout the water.

5. Place the deckle (open frame) on the mold (frame with screen) and slowly lower it into the container filled with water, pulp and botanicals (A). After the pulp flows over the mold, lift out of the container keeping it level. After a few seconds tilt to drain off remaining water.

6. Set the deckle and mold on the table (B). Take off the deckle and put a piece of felt on top of the paper that is on the mold and turn over carefully onto a table surface.

7. Use the sponge and press on the screen to remove water from the paper. (C) Squeeze out the sponge often to get as much water out of the paper sheet as possible. Then slowly lift the mold leaving the paper on the felt. (D).

8. Once paper is transferred to the felt, put another piece of felt on top (E) and use the rolling pin to extract out more water (F). Another way of extracting the water is to stack sets of felts with paper sandwiched between and put them between two boards and apply a heavy object on top.

9. When the water is extracted, take off the top piece of felt and turn over the felt with the piece of paper onto a smooth glass or plastic surface. Slowly peel back the felt removing it from the paper. When the paper is dry peel it slowly off of the surface.

10. Flatten the paper by ironing the side with fewer botanicals (G).

11. Make your own bookmarks (H), greetings cards or envelopes by using existing envelopes as a guide for the shape.

# DEVELOPING FLOWER MOTIFS

*Words and photos by Louise Gale*

Capture the timeless beauty of the life cycle of a flower.

## "Every flower blooms in its own time."

### - Ken Petti

When I draw in my sketchbook, one of my favourite ways to attune myself to nature is to capture the beauty of a single flower at various stages of its life. I use this process to deeply connect to the present moment and tap into an endless source of inspiration for drawing motifs for my botanical mandala artwork.

A motif is a decorative image or design (especially a repeated one) that forms a pattern. Over the years I have developed a precious collection of motif sketches and mini paintings that are inspired by the botanical world.

Whether you are new to sketching, would like to dive deeper into nature drawing or are keen to explore flower art such as creating botanical mandalas, I hope these tips will inspire you to observe a single flower in more detail through its own cycle of time.

Let's take the Dahlia as an example. At every stage of growth there is a different shape, variations in colour and lots of details to capture. When we start to look closely, we can begin to notice variations within a flower species and the infinite beauty that nature provides.

PLANTS ARE MAGIC #3 TIME

# Draw the flowers

1. Choose a flower that you are drawn to today or start with your favourite flower.
2. Take one flower from the plant to observe. Look at the shapes and colours. What stage of growth is it at compared to the others?
3. Capture its beauty from different perspectives. Hold the flower to one side, upside down, look at it from above, from below and from the side. Select other flowers or stems that show different stages from bud through to full bloom.
4. Sketch out the shapes and see how many motifs or sketchbook pages you can create from this one single flower species.
5. Capture the colour palette for colour inspiration and future reference.

# Make a mandala

Once you have finished drawing and observing your living plant, honour it by arranging the petals into a mandala. To capture its timeless beauty, preserve the flowers and petals by pressing them.

*Louise's new book 'Botanical Mandalas' is out now. Visit: botanicalmandalas.com.*

"Society grows great when wise
(wo)men plant trees whose shade
they know they shall never sit in."

- Greek Proverb

# MAGNOLIA

*Words and photo by Ellie Beck*

## "...OUR ACTIONS UPON THIS EARTH AFFECT GENERATIONS TO COME."

In my garden we have a giant magnolia tree, planted by my mother almost 40 years ago. In the scale of the life of a tree, 40 is not very many years, but my mother did not have the privilege of growing old to sit under this tree. My children now climb this tree.

When she planted this tree, I'm sure my mother did not ponder the future of herself or even of the tree. Of course, I'm speculating here, but would she have guessed that her future grandchildren would play *'Who can climb the highest'*? Did she imagine them hiding deep in the branches where no one could find them, or use it as a place to run away to when they needed protection and felt like sulking or being alone?

The grandchildren she would never meet now climb adventurously through the branches of the tree-of-life, without her

by their side. The grandchildren who would only know her by the stories that her own children have told them. The memories shared are of a woman wise beyond anything they knew.

Even though my mother and father planted many trees upon this property where I now live with my children, it is this magnolia that brings me the biggest joys and bittersweet tinges. While I don't have strong childhood memories of this particular magnolia (though there were others), it is now as a motherless-mother whose own children climb, play, sing, call, scamper, adventure among the branches, I am reminded that our actions upon this earth affect generations to come. My mother was never able to climb this now giant tree herself, but her grandchildren do, and with that action they bring her memory back to us each day. 🌿

Plants Are Magic is an independent magazine
for makers, dreamers & plant lovers.

Editor, creative director & publisher:
REBECCA DESNOS

web:        www.rebeccadesnos.com
email:      info@rebeccadesnos.com

Front & back cover photos by Rebecca Desnos
Photo of white flowers on first page by Annie Spratt

Logo by Inge van Geem

Sources of items on front cover
Mug: etsy.com/shop/viCeramics
Pressed flower art: etsy.com/shop/shoppalyglass

Second edition ISBN 978-0-9955566-5-2

Published by Rebecca Desnos, in 2019, in the UK.

First edition (2018) ISSN 2514-2143
Digital edition: ISSN 2514-2151

Disclaimer

The opinions expressed in Plants Are Magic do not
necessarily represent those of the publisher. Whilst
the publisher takes every care in checking the
validity of information given in articles and other
contributions, it cannot accept legal responsibility
for its accuracy or liability for any form of damages
incurred by the use of such information.  The
content is for informational purposes only.
The information in Plants Are Magic has not
been evaluated by the Medicines & Healthcare
Products Regulatory Agency or the Food & Drug
Administration. This information is not intended to
diagnose, treat, cure, or prevent any disease.